I0490311

Forex Ai Cross System

Mark Digitalis

Contents

1 The System

2 Introduction

3 Where to Trade

4 When to Trade

5 What to Trade

6 Afterword

7 Forex in Few Words

8 Disclaimer

9 BONUS

The System

Forex Ai Cross Sytem is designed for the people who already know trading technologies on stock, commodity, futures, and currency markets; the knowledge of basic notions in technical analysis of these markets is also required.

If you are not aware of the above-mentioned notions, you should master their basics.

Introduction

Whether you wish to become a successful trader, or you already are a professional in this field, this information will be of enormous value for you in any case.

There are lots of opinions and points of view on: how trade operations should be made, what markets to choose, when should the trades be opened and closed, what analytical methods give best results, etc.

The variety of opinions can be represented in one idea - the markets are constantly fluctuating, giving the possibility to earn money for one part of traders and, unfortunately, to lose the money for another part.

Though the number of disputable points of view on this problem is very high, all of them try to find answers to the three questions:

Where to trade?

When to trade?

What to trade?

Forex Ai Cross Sytem will give you the answers to these questions, enabling you to earn stable income on regular basis.

Where to Trade

Today one of the most attractive places for speculative trades among other markets is Foreign Exchange Currency Market. It is the largest market in the world with the daily turnover of $1.5 trillion. This exceeds many times the daily turnover of the world's largest exchanges.

Forex is not represented by a single exchange: it is functioning through the electronic net, connecting large banks, numerous funds, international corporations, and brokerage houses.

All the day round the exchange of different world currencies is performed on Forex.

Forex used to be available only for those who were able to spend hundreds of thousands of US dollars.

The swift development of Internet technologies gave a possibility for individual investors with small capital to trade on Forex directly from their own computers.

A trader with small capital can get the necessary informational support on trade related issues on the same level as all the largest participants of this markets.

As the daylight wakes the cities of Tokyo, Hong Kong, Singapore, Bombay, Frankfurt, Zurich, London, New York, the financial centers of New Zealand and Australia; they start the great global rush for profits on Forex.

24 hours a day.

5 days a week.

Daily turnover of $1.5 trillion.

Superliquidity.

The usage of leverage trading.

Possibility to make profits both on «bullish» and «bearish» markets.

ALL THIS IS FOREX

No other market in the world gives you such great variety of possibilities as Forex.

The answer to "Where to trade?" is evident.

For getting the maximum profits in speculative business I recommend trading on Forex.

When to Trade

Selecting the moment for opening and closing positions is one of the most difficult tasks. For many centuries specialists tried to create various theories, methods, and approaches.

This notwithstanding, market seems to take little notice of the opinions of the so-called "analytics".

The king of the market is price, which absorbs the emotions of millions of people, the economies of hundreds of countries, sophisticated indicators, numerous support and resistance lines.

You can succeed on the market only when you do not go against the price.

That is why price following is the real source of stable income.

One of the most well spread tools of determining market movements is the method of moving averages.

There are three types of moving averages: (1)simple, (2) exponential, and (3) weighted.

The strong point of these indicators is that they show the trends of market movements on their early stages.

The major parameter for moving average is its window. The size of windows depends upon the goals of the analysis performed by the specialists.

It needs no proving that exponential moving average (EMA) serves as an effective support/resistance line and shows good results on charts with different time intervals.

Open on your trading platform the 1 hour chart of any currency pair (e.g. EUR/USD) and set EMA indicator (Exponential Moving Average) with the period of24.

Make careful examination of current price movements.

Now imagine that you left your working place and returned 24 hours later. When you came back, you saw that the market remained on its place.

Actually, it could be this way. But only if no information (at all) came to the market within this period of time.

INDICATORS

A good understanding of the basic tenets of technical analysis can vastly improve one's trading skills.

When using technical analysis, price is the primary tool. Simply put, "everything is already in the rate." However, technical analysis involves a bit more than simply staring at price charts hoping to find a "yellow brick road" to a bonanza payday. Along with various methods of plotting price action on charts by using bars, candlesticks, and Xs and Os on point and figure charts, market technicians also employ many technical studies that help them to delve deeper into the data. By using these studies in conjunction with their price charts, traders are able to build much stronger cases to buy, sell or remain on the sidelines than they could by simply looking at price charts alone.

Here are descriptions of some of the more widely used and time-tested studies that technicians keep in their toolboxes:

Indicators

Moving Averages

Stochastics

RSI

Bollinger Bands

MACD

Fibonacci

Moving Averages

One of the most basic and widely used indicators in a technical analyst's tool box, moving averages help traders verify existing trends, identify emerging trends, and view overextended trends about to reverse. Moving averages are lines overlaid on a chart indicating long term price trends with short term fluctuations smoothed out.

There are three basic types of moving averages:

Simple

Weighted

Exponential

A simple moving average gives equal weight to each price point over the specified period. The user defines whether the high, low, or close is used and these price points are added together and averaged. This average price point is then added to the existing string and a line is formed. With the addition of each new price point the sample set drops off the oldest point. The simple moving average is probably the most widely used moving average.

A weighted moving average gives more emphasis to the latest data. A weighted moving average multiplies each data point by a weighting factor which differs from day to day. These figures are added and divided by the sum of the weighting factors. A weighted moving average allows the user to successfully smooth out a curve while having the average more responsive to current price changes.

An exponential moving average is another way of "weighting" the more recent data. An exponential moving average multiplies a percentage of the most recent price by the previous period's average price. Defining the optimum moving average for a particular currency pair involves "curve fitting". Curve fitting is the process of selecting the right number of periods with the correct type of moving average to produce the results the user is trying to achieve. By trial and error, technicians work with the time periods to fit the price data. Because the moving average is constantly changing based on the latest market data, many traders will use different "specified" time frames before they come up with a series of moving averages that are optimal for a particular currency.

For example, a trader might create a 5-day, a 15-day and a 30-day moving average for a currency and then plot them on his or her price chart. He might start out using simple moving averages and end up using weighted moving averages. In creating these moving averages, traders need to decide on the exact price data that will be used in this study; meaning closing prices vs. opening prices vs. high/low/close etc. After doing so, a series of lines are created that reflect the 5-day, 15-day and 30-day moving average of a currency.

Once the data is layered over a price chart, traders can determine how well these chosen periods keep track of the trend being followed. If, for example, a market is trending higher, you'd expect the 30-day moving average to be a very accurate trend line, providing a line of support for prices on their way higher. If prices seem too close under this 30-day moving average on several occasions without resulting in a halt in the up trend, a trader will simply adjust the time period to say a 45-day or 60-day moving average in order to optimize the average. In this way, the moving average will act as a trend line.

After determining the optimum moving average for a currency, this average price line can be used as a line of support in maintaining a long position or resistance in maintaining a short position. Breaches of this line can also be used as a signal that a currency is in the process of reversing course, in which case a trader will want to pare back an existing position or come up with entry levels for a new position. For example, if you determine that a 30-day moving average has shown itself to be a good support line for USD-JPY in an upward trending market, then market closes under this 30-day moving average line could be a signal that this trend could be running out of steam. However, it is important to wait for confirmation of these signals. One way to do this is to wait for another close below the level. On the second close under the average, you should begin to pare down your position. Another confirmation involves using other, shorter term moving averages.

While a longer term moving average can help to define and support a particular trend, shorter term moving averages can provide lead signals that a trend is ending before prices dip below your longer term moving average line. For this reason, most traders will plot several moving averages on the same chart. In a market that is trending higher, a shorter term moving average might signal a market reversal by turning down and crossing over the longer term moving average. For example, if you are using a 15-day and a 45-day moving average in a market that is in an up trend, and the 15-day moving average turns down and crosses over the 45-day moving average, this could be an early signal that the up trend is ending and it is probably time to begin to pare down your position. (Back to Indicators)

Stochastics

Stochastic studies, or oscillators, are another useful tool for monitoring the expected sustainability of a trend. They provide a trader with information about the closing price in the current trading period relative to the prior performance of the instrument being analyzed.

Stochastics are measured and represented by two different lines, %K and %D and are plotted on a scale ranging from 0 to 100. Indications above 80 represent strong upward movement while level indications below 20 represent strong downward movements. The mathematics behind
the studies are not as important as knowing what the stochastics are telling you. The %K line is the faster, more sensitive indicator while the %D line takes more time to turn. When the %K line crosses over the %D line, this could be an indication that a market is about to reverse course. Stochastic studies are not useful in choppy, sideways markets. At times when prices are fluctuating in a narrow range, the %K and %D lines might be crossing many different times and will be telling you nothing more than the market is moving sideways. Stochastics are most useful in measuring the strength of a trend and as augurs of a coming reversal in prices. When prices are making new highs or lows and your stochastics are doing the same, you can be reasonably certain that the trend will continue. On the other hand, many traders finds that the best trading opportunity comes when their stochastic indicator is flattening out or moving in the opposite direction of prices. When these divergences

occur, it's time to book profits and/or to establish a position in the opposite direction of the prior trend.

As should always be the case when using any technical tool, do not act on the first signal you see. Wait at least one or two trading sessions for confirmation of what the study is indicating before you commit to a position. (Back to Indicators)

Relative Strength Index (RSI)

RSI measures the momentum of price movements. It is also plotted on a scale ranging from 0 to 100. Traders will tend to look at RSI readings over 80 as an indicator of a market that is overbought or susceptible to a downturn, and readings under 20 as a market that is oversold or ready to turn higher.

This logic therefore implies that prices cannot rise or fall forever and that by using an RSI study, one can determine with a reasonable degree of certainty when a reversal will come about. However, be very wary of trading on RSI studies alone. In many instances, an RSI can remain at very lofty or sunken levels for quite a while without prices reversing course. At these times, the RSI is simply telling you that a market is quite strong or quite weak and shows no signs of changing course.

RSI studies can be adjusted to whatever time sensitivity a trader feels necessary for his or her particular style. For instance, a 5-day RSI will be very sensitive and will tend to give many more signals, not all of them sustainable, than say a 21-day RSI, which will tend to be less choppy. As with other studies, try a variety of time periods for the currency that you are trading based on your trading style. Longer term, position type traders, will tend to find that shorter time frames used for an RSI (or any other study for that matter) will give too many signals and will result in over-trading. On the other hand, shorter time frames will probably be ideal for day-traders trying to capture many shorter-term price fluctuations.

As with stochastics, look for divergences between prices and the RSI. If your RSI turns up in a slumping market or turns down during a bull run, this could be a good indication that a reversal is just around the corner. Wait for confirmation before you act on divergent indications from your RSI studies. (Back to Indicators)

Bollinger Bands

Bollinger Bands are volatility curves used to identify extreme highs or lows in relation to price. Bollinger Bands establish trading parameters, or bands, based on the moving average of a particular instrument and a set number of standard deviations around this moving average.

For example, a trader might decide to use a 10-day moving average and 2 standard deviations to establish Bollinger Bands for a given currency. After doing so, a chart will appear with price bars capped by an upper boundary line based on price levels 2 standard deviations higher than the 10-day moving average and supported by a lower boundary line based on 2 standard deviations lower than the 10-day moving average. In the middle of these two boundary lines will be another line running somewhat close to the middle area depicting in this case, the 10-day moving average. Both the moving average and the number of standard deviations can be altered to best suit a particular currency.

Jon Bollinger, creator of Bollinger Bands recommends using a simple 20-day moving average and 2 standard deviations. Because standard deviation is a measure of volatility, Bollinger Bands are dynamic indicators that adjust themselves (widen and contract) based on the current levels of volatility in the market being studied. When prices hit the upper or lower boundaries of a given set of Bollinger Bands, this is not necessarily an indication of an imminent reversal in a trend. It simply means that prices have moved to the upper limits of the established parameters. Therefore, traders should use another study in conjunction with Bollinger Bands to help them determine the strength of a trend. (Back to Indicators)

MACD - Moving Average Convergence Divergence

MACD is a more detailed method of using moving averages to find trading signals from price charts. Developed by Gerald Appel, the MACD plots the difference between a 26-day exponential moving average and a 12-day exponential moving average. A 9-day moving average is generally used as a trigger line, meaning when the MACD crosses below this trigger it is a bearish signal and when it crosses above it, it's a bullish signal.

As with other studies, traders will look to MACD studies to provide early signals or

divergences between market prices and a technical indicator. If the MACD turns positive and makes higher lows while prices are still tanking, this could be a strong buy signal.

Conversely, if the MACD makes lower highs while prices are making new highs, this could be a strong bearish divergence and a sell signal. (Back to Indicators)

Fibonacci Retracements

Fibonacci retracement levels are a sequence of numbers discovered by the noted mathematician

Leonardo da Pisa during the twelfth century. These numbers describe cycles found throughout nature and when applied to technical analysis can be used to find pullbacks in the currency

market. Fibonacci retracement involves anticipating changes in trends as prices near the lines created by the Fibonacci studies. After a significant price move (either up or down), prices will often retrace a significant portion (if not all) of the original move. As prices retrace, support and resistance levels often occur at or near the Fibonacci Retracement levels.

In the currency markets, the commonly used sequence of ratios is 23.6 %, 38.2%, 50% and

61.8%. Fibonacci retracement levels can easily be displayed by connecting a trend line from

a perceived high point to a perceived low point. By taking the difference between the high

and low, the user can apply the % ratios to achieve the desired pullbacks.

One final word of advice: Don't get too caught up in the mathematics involved in putting

together each study. It is much more important to understand how and why studies can and

should be manipulated based on the time periods and sensitivities that you determine are

ideal for the currency you are trading. These ideal levels can only be determined after

applying several different parameters to each study until the charts and studies begin to reveal the "details behind the details."

Set up another EMA24 (chose its color to be different from the previous EMA) with the time shift to24 hours ahead.

This indicator will show the situation on the market in 24 hours as if no new information has reached it.

But in reality the market is "alive". It moves constantly, and the picture it will get in 24 hours has great chances to differ from the picture of our indicatorEMA24(+24).

Now I would like to draw your attention to the gap betweenEMA24 and EMA24(+24).

I called this gap an "Ai Cross".

The core of my system is the following: it is possible to make decisions about necessary market actions after analyzing the way (how and when) current prices overcome "Ai Cross's".

When to Trade

Selecting the moment for opening and closing positions is one of the most difficult tasks. For many centuries specialists tried to create various theories, methods, and approaches.

This notwithstanding, market seems to take little notice of the opinions of the so-called "analytics".

The king of the market is price, which absorbs the emotions of millions of people, the economies of hundreds of countries, sophisticated indicators, numerous support and resistance lines.

You can succeed on the market only when you do not go against the price.

That is why price following is the real source of stable

income.

One of the most well spread tools of determining market movements is the method of moving averages.

There are three types of moving averages: (1)simple, (2) exponential, and (3) weighted.

The strong point of these indicators is that they show the trends of market movements on their early stages.

The major parameter for moving average is its window. The size of windows depends upon the goals of the analysis performed by the specialists.

It needs no proving that exponential moving average (EMA) serves as an effective support/resistance line and shows good results on charts with different time intervals.

Open on your trading platform the 1 hour chart of any currency pair (e.g. EUR/USD) and set EMA indicator (Exponential Moving Average) with the period of24.

Make careful examination of current price movements.

Now imagine that you left your working place and returned 24 hours later. When you came back, you saw that the market remained on its place.

Actually, it could be this way. But only if no information (at all) came to the market within this period of time.

sis for defining entry/exit points should be done is given below.

Set up one more indicator: **Fractal**.

This indicator should be on any trading platform under the same name.

This indicator was invented by Bill Williams.

It is worth mentioning that Williams's definition of this indicator - made on the basis of fractal geometry this sphere of science - is not very correct.

The founder of fractal geometry Benoit Mandelbrot defined fractal as:

"A fractal is a geometric shape that can be separated into parts, each of which is areduced-scale version of the whole."

(Fractals and Scaling in Finance: Discontinuity, Concentration, Risk. Benoit Mandelbrot. Springer-Verlag, 1997.)

I would call the formations of such kind as "Market Breather".

However, the existing name for the phenomenon already exists and is widely used.

That is why I will continue using the term "fractal" the way it was given by Bill Williams.

Fractal is a model of (at least) five consequent bars when the central bar reaches maximum/minimum.

Here go the examples of such fractal models:

a - up fractal; b - down fractal; c & d - void fractals.

Under the Ai Cross trading system the fractals,

• when central bars are the maximums and minimums in the model at the same time (see picture 'd');

• when minimum and maximum belong to neighboring bars (see picture 'c') ,

will be viewed as void fractals.

On successful finishing of the first three steps we have already got all the tools of technical analysis necessary for proper usage of my system.

The position should be opened when the prices have overcome "Ai Cross".

• When the prices overcome "Ai Cross" from below, the buy position should be opened at the price of one pips above the level of previous active (not void!) fractal.

• When the prices overcome "Ai Cross" from above, the sell position should be opened at the price of one pips below the level of previous active (not void!)

fractal.

You can see the way these rules work in reality on these pictures:

Crucial Rules

As we have successfully passed the previous four steps we can easily start learning crucial trading rules. Make sure that you have learned them carefully before starting the trades.

1. When the position is opened, the stop loss order is immediately set up on the level of 50 pips from the entry point.

2. When opening/closing any position, the switch/reversal technique should be used (i.e. alongside with closing the position we should open a new position at the price defined in Step 4).

3. Never open buy position below EMA24(+24) or sell position aboveEMA24(+24). Only exception from this rule is the case when position is closed with stop loss order

4. Close old position/open new position at the price one pips below (for selling) or one pips above (for buying) the level of the last (not previous!) active fractal, heading in opposite direction to the currently opened position in cases when:

• within one hour the market passed more than75 pips or gap took place; in this case you can still exit at the price of one pip better the entry point;

• 2-3 void fractals occur in consequence (one after another);

• during the period when the position was opened not a single fractal headed in opposite direction to the position appeared;

• the signal of the previous active fractal cannot be executed (which may happen in situation of Rule #3).

• during the period when the position was opened market made more than250

pips.

Capital Management

It is important not only to define properly the entry/exit points in trading. Another

significant issue is to use your capital wisely. In other words, you will need to know how

many contracts should be traded in each case.

Before making any calculations you have to define your risk level or the sum which you

are ready to risk at any transaction. The risk level is represented in percentage (%) from

your balance.

I use risk level of 5-20% depending upon the desire of clients when I trade their

capitals. When my personal funds are traded, I usually set risk level at 10%.

As you remember from the previous rules, when any position is opened, the stop loss is

placed immediately at 50 pips from the entry point. That is why the maximum potential

loss on one contract of USD/CHFis about $375.

Now you have defined necessary values and can calculate the number of contracts to be

traded: If your trading platform allows to trade fractional lots, the result of the calculation

should be rounded off to one digit after the dot.

If you have not got such option, round off the result to the full integer.

This example will illustrate you how to use the formula. Let's say, my account balance is

$10,000 and risk level is10%:

Crucial Note to Limit Losses

I advise stop trading when current losses exceed 40% of the account balance at the

beginning of the month. The losses of such level show that market is moving too chaotically to be traded. You should better wait until the beginning of next month which will compensate your losses.

Another important moment - which can make the system even more effective - is the usage of rules to add the position when the market moves as expected.

You should add to the position after the prices overcome the fractal (if it goes in the same direction with the position opened) which has been created by the movement of market since this position was opened.

To make proper addition to the position, you should stick to these rules:

• open not more than 3 positions in one direction;

• each added position should be equal in size to the first position (opened in this direction);

• usually a fractal (headed in opposite direction to the position) should take place between the additions, and it top/bottom should be one pip below/above the previous entry point; this rule may be neglected if you think that the prices are close to significant level (when this level is broken through this will cause great movement);

• **DO NOT** add to the position if:

a) the market has passed more than 200 pips;

b) EMA24 and EMA24(+24) have crossed for several times during the currently opened position;

c) the addition is initiated by the fractals which are below (for buying) or above (for selling) the last fractal in the direction of the opened position;

d) the market has "stuck" on the same place, having caused several fractals to be nearly on the same level.

How to Organize Trading Process Properly

After learning all the rules I advise you to open a demo account and try "Ai Cross" SYSTEM in practice. On demo account you risk nothing and see the way system works.

It may seem that 1 hour charts require market monitoring for24 hours a day. But it is not true.

The signals created by the system occur every10-12 hours . After testing the system on demo account you will learn how to place the orders for opening/closing position properly. Using the instructions of your trading platform you will pass the "adaptation" stage quickly.

Please note that orders should be placed only when their price is higher (for buying) or lower (for selling) than EMA24(+24). You should draw a line at the level of your potential entry point and look for its crossover with EMA24(+24). You can easily do it as EMA24(+24) will allow you to be ahead of the market on 24 hours. The orders placed before the proper time can result in wrong trading actions.

It should also be mentioned that if your charts are built on BID prices, you should remember about spread when placing orders.

For example, the charts reach the level of 1.3400 (BID), the fractal appears and you decide to place order: the purchase price of this order is made of the buying price itself (1.3401) + spread offered by your broker.

You will also learn to assess current market situation and make changes in order placement with all referring calculations taking about5 minutes.

To my mind, after about two weeks of successful practice you may start real trading with **Ai Cross** SYSTEM, spending only several hours a day on it.

I can provide some additional details to help create a trading manual for traders who are willing to use this system.

Finding Trending Stocks or Commodities:

To identify trending stocks or commodities, traders can use technical analysis tools like moving averages and trendlines. A stock or commodity with a clear uptrend or downtrend is more likely to generate profitable trading signals. It's important to select stocks or commodities that have sufficient trading volume and liquidity to ensure that trades can be executed efficiently and with minimal slippage.

Identifying Crossovers:

EMA24 and EMA24(+24) can be used to identify potential buy and sell signals. When the EMA24 crosses above the EMA24(+24), it indicates a potential buy signal, while a cross below could indicate a potential sell signal. Traders can also use other indicators such as RSI or MACD to confirm these signals and avoid false signals.

Confirming Signals with the Williams Fractal Indicator:

Once a potential buy or sell signal is generated using EMA24 and EMA24(+24), traders can use the Williams Fractal indicator to confirm the signal. A buy signal is confirmed when the highest high of the fractal appears above the previous highest high, while a sell signal is confirmed when the lowest low of the fractal appears below the previous lowest low. This confirmation helps to avoid false signals and increases the probability of a profitable trade.

Entering a Long or Short Position:

Once the buy or sell signal is confirmed, traders can enter a long or short position. They can use various order types like market, limit or stop-limit orders to enter the position at the desired price. It's important to place a stop loss order to limit potential losses in case the trade goes against the trader's expectations.

Monitoring the Position:

Traders should monitor the position regularly to ensure that it is performing as expected. They can use various technical analysis tools to set profit targets or identify potential exit signals. For example, they can exit the position when the EMA24 and EMA24(+24) cross in the opposite direction or when a fractal in the opposite direction appears.

Managing Risk:

Managing risk is crucial in trading. Traders should always use stop-loss orders to limit potential losses and use position sizing to manage their risk exposure. They should also be aware of market news and events that could affect the stock or commodity they are trading and adjust their positions accordingly.

In summary, the trading system using EMA24, EMA24(+24), and the Williams Fractal indicator can be a profitable strategy for traders willing to take on the risk of trading. By combining these indicators and following the steps outlined in this trading manual, traders can increase the probability of making profitable trades while managing their risk exposure. However, traders should always do their own research and analysis before making any investment decisions.

The Trade

EMA (Exponential Moving Average) is a type of moving average that gives more weight to recent price data, making it more responsive to changes in price trends. EMA24 refers to a 24-period exponential moving average.

The Williams Fractal trading indicator is a technical analysis tool used to identify potential reversal points in price trends. It consists of a series of five consecutive bars, where the middle bar has the highest high or lowest low, surrounded by two lower highs and two higher lows.

To combine these indicators, you could use the following trading system:

Look for stocks or commodities with a clear trend in either direction.

Use EMA24 and EMA24(+24) to identify crossovers. When the EMA24 crosses above the EMA24(+24), it could indicate a buy signal, and when the EMA24 crosses below the EMA24(+24), it could indicate a sell signal.

Once a buy or sell signal is triggered, look for confirmation using the Williams Fractal indicator. A buy signal is confirmed when the highest high of the fractal appears above the previous highest high, and a sell signal is confirmed when the lowest low of the fractal appears below the previous lowest low.

Enter a long or short position based on the confirmed signal and place a stop loss order to limit potential losses.

Monitor the position and exit when the EMA24 and EMA24(+24) cross in the opposite direction, or when a fractal in the opposite direction appears. and create a trading manual for traders willing to take on the risk or profit and loss

The system provided above can be used with various time intervals and currency pairs.

However, my trading experience and objective results showed that the most stable flow

of income generated by the system was made on the pair of EUR/USD on 1 hour charts.

These results are explained by the following factors:

• USD has the " Save-Haven Status "

Central Bank in providing its monetary policy and guarantees safety of

information about clients' deposits.

• DOLLAR trend is more stable compared to other currencies.

• Volatility of EUR enables one to make money on it nearly every day.

• The size of fluctuations during 1 hour and the peculiarity of fractal formations

for this currency pair gives possibility to trade even small sums starting with

$1,000 on it. On the other side, successful trading with 4 hours and daily charts

will require increase of stop loss size and huge sums of money, exceeding

thousands and hundreds of thousands.

I can provide a hypothetical example of a trade based on the system outlined earlier.

Let's say you identified a clear upward trend in the NASDAQ and decided to use the trading
system outlined earlier to enter a long position.

You place a buy order for $10,000 when the EMA24 crosses above the EMA24(+24), indicating a
potential buy signal. You set a stop loss order at a level that you are comfortable with to limit
potential losses.

As the day progresses, the NASDAQ continues to rise, and you notice that a fractal appears with
the middle bar having the highest high and surrounded by two lower highs and two higher lows,
confirming the buy signal.

You continue to monitor the position and eventually close the trade when the EMA24 crosses
below the EMA24(+24), indicating a potential sell signal, or when a fractal appears with the

middle bar having the lowest low and surrounded by two higher lows and two lower highs, indicating a potential reversal.

Assuming you closed the trade at a profit, you could potentially earn a return on investment. However, the specific outcome of the trade would depend on a variety of factors, including market conditions, asset volatility, and individual trading decisions.

It could be possible to use a trading bot to perform the Forex Ai Crosss System tasks successfully for you so see below a sample script for a trading bot that implements the trading system discussed earlier who wishes to **LONG** the market (they hope the price will go up) . However, please note that this script is for educational purposes only and should not be used for live trading without proper testing and validation.

```python
# Import necessary libraries

import pandas as pd

import numpy as np

import talib

import ccxt
```

```python
# Set up the exchange
exchange = ccxt.binance({
    'apiKey': 'YOUR_API_KEY',
    'secret': 'YOUR_SECRET_KEY',
})

# Set up the trading pair
symbol = 'BTC/USDT'

# Set up the trading parameters
position_size = 0.01 # the size of the position to take
stop_loss = 0.02 # the percentage to use as a stop loss
take_profit = 0.02 # the percentage to use as a take profit

# Set up the indicator parameters
ema_period = 24
fractal_period = 5

# Set up the trading bot function
def trading_bot():
    # Get the historical data
    data = exchange.fetch_ohlcv(symbol, timeframe='1d')
    df = pd.DataFrame(data, columns=['timestamp', 'open', 'high', 'low', 'close', 'volume'])
    df['timestamp'] = pd.to_datetime(df['timestamp'], unit='ms')
    df.set_index('timestamp', inplace=True)
```

```python
# Calculate the indicators
df['ema24'] = talib.EMA(df['close'], timeperiod=ema_period)
df['ema24_plus_24'] = talib.EMA(df['close'], timeperiod=ema_period) + 24
df['fractal'] = talib.CDLFRACALL(df['high'], df['low'], df['close'], df['open'], penetration=0)


# Initialize the trading variables
position = None
buy_price = None
stop_loss_price = None
take_profit_price = None


# Loop through the data and execute trades
for i in range(fractal_period, len(df)):
    # Check for a buy signal
    if df['ema24'][i] > df['ema24_plus_24'][i] and df['fractal'][i] > 0:
        if position is None:
            # Open a long position
            position = 'long'
            buy_price = df['close'][i]
            stop_loss_price = buy_price * (1 - stop_loss)
            take_profit_price = buy_price * (1 + take_profit)
            exchange.create_market_buy_order(symbol, position_size)
            print(f'Opened long position at {buy_price}')
        else:
```

```python
        # Increase the position size

        exchange.create_market_buy_order(symbol, position_size)

        print(f'Increased long position at {df["close"][i]}')
    # Check for a sell signal
    elif df['ema24'][i] < df['ema24_plus_24'][i] and df['fractal'][i] < 0:
        if position is None:
            # Open a short position
            position = 'short'
            sell_price = df['close'][i]
            stop_loss_price = sell_price * (1 + stop_loss)
            take_profit_price = sell_price * (1 - take_profit)
            exchange.create_market_sell_order(symbol, position_size)
            print(f'Opened short position at {sell_price}')
        else:
            # Increase the position size
            exchange.create_market_sell_order(symbol, position_size)
            print(f'Increased short position at {df["close"][i]}')
    # Check for a stop loss or take profit
    elif position == 'long':
```

_____ -

And here is another script for the Forex Ai Cross System Bot for a trader who wishes to **SHORT** the market (they hope the prices will fall)

_____ -

Import necessary libraries

```python
import pandas as pd

import talib

import oandapyV20

from oandapyV20 import API

from oandapyV20.exceptions import V20Error

from oandapyV20.endpoints.instruments import InstrumentsCandles


# Set up Oanda API connection

accountID = "YOUR_ACCOUNT_ID"

access_token = "YOUR_ACCESS_TOKEN"

api = API(access_token=access_token, environment="practice")


# Define trading parameters

instrument = "NAS100_USD" # Change this to the instrument you want to trade

units = 1000 # Number of units to trade

stop_loss = 50 # Stop loss in pips

take_profit = 100 # Take profit in pips


# Define function to get market data

def get_market_data(instrument):

    params = {"count": 1000, "granularity": "M5"}

    candles = InstrumentsCandles(instrument=instrument, params=params)

    try:

        api.request(candles)

    except V20Error as e:
```

```python
            print("Error: {}".format(e))
    else:
        data = candles.response["candles"]
        df = pd.DataFrame(data)
        df["time"] = pd.to_datetime(df["time"])
        df.set_index("time", inplace=True)
        df.drop(["complete", "volume"], axis=1, inplace=True)
        df.columns = ["open", "high", "low", "close"]
        df = df.astype(float)
        return df


# Define function to calculate EMA24 and EMA24(+24)
def calculate_ema(df):
    ema24 = talib.EMA(df["close"], timeperiod=24)
    ema24_plus24 = talib.EMA(df["close"], timeperiod=48)
    return ema24, ema24_plus24


# Define function to calculate Williams Fractal
def calculate_fractal(df):
    fractal = talib.CDLFRACTAL(df["high"], df["low"])
    return fractal


# Define function to place a trade
def place_trade(instrument, units, stop_loss, take_profit):
    order = {
```

```python
    "order": {

      "units": str(units),

      "instrument": instrument,

      "timeInForce": "FOK",

      "type": "MARKET",

      "positionFill": "DEFAULT",

      "stopLossOnFill": {

        "timeInForce": "GTC",

        "price": str(stop_loss)

      },

      "takeProfitOnFill": {

        "timeInForce": "GTC",

        "price": str(take_profit)

      }

    }

  }
  try:

    api.request(oandapyV20.endpoints.orders.OrderCreate(accountID, data=order))
  except V20Error as e:

    print("Error: {}".format(e))


# Define function to close a trade

def close_trade(tradeID):

  try:

    api.request(oandapyV20.endpoints.trades.TradeClose(accountID=accountID,
tradeID=tradeID))
```

```
    except V20Error as e:

      print("Error: {}".format(e))


# Define main function for the trading bot

def main():

  while True:

    # Get market data

    df = get_market_data(instrument)


    # Calculate EMA24 and EMA24(+24)

    ema24, ema24_plus24 = calculate_ema(df)


    # Calculate Williams Fractal

    fractal = calculate_fractal(df)


    # Check if
```

Again , please note that this script is for educational purposes only and should not be used for live trading without proper testing and validation.

Afterword

Periods for EMA and the number defining the size of "Ai Cross" were taken not

occasionally. Various combinations of numbers were tested for effectivity, and it turned out that the number - 24- fitted the system perfectly.

REMEMBER: even the best trading system will not spare you the necessity to work.

Only the combination of your devotion to work, self-control, and discipline will make

successful basis for getting stable income with the Ai Cross SYSTEM.

FOREX in Few Words

Forex (Foreign currency Exchange market) is an interbank currency market which

major function is to provide currencies exchange between banks of different countries.

The rate of exchange is the price of the monetary unit of one country, represented in the

monetary units on another country.

The agents of market, responsible for operating with market quotations on

buying/selling different currencies and responsible for making real trades on these

currencies, are called market-makers.

The agents of market, who create the demand for the certain currency rates, are called

market-users.

The relations between market-makers and market-users are performed through the

mediation of brokerage companies.

The currency quotation looks the following way:

USD/CHF=1.3560/64

This means that trader can buy USDat the bid price of CHF 1.3564, and sell USD at the

ask price of CHF 1.3560.

The least possible price change is called a pip.

1 pip=0.0001

The essence of speculative trades on Forex lies in getting income from changes of rates.

The graphic visualizations of market movements are called charts.

The are different ways for graphical representation of price changes at a certain time interval.

These major ways are:

Bar Charts

Four prices are determined for each time interval:

Open (opening price), Close(closing price), High (the highest price), Low (the lowest price).

CandleStick Charts If opening price is lower than the closing price, the body of the candle is white. If opening price is higher than the closing price, the body of the candle is black.

The following analytical methods are used for determining market movements:

• fundamental (the analysis of key macro economic indexes for the state of the national economy; these indexes influence both the level of currency rate and the market competitors);

• technical (method of prices investigation based on charts and various indicators which are calculated from 'state of the market' information).

The results of market analysis make the core for a trading plan. The plan's key elements are:

1. The currency to be traded.

2. The trading operation to be performed: buy or sell.

3. The price to enter the market (opening position price).

4. The price to leave the market (closing position price) if the position continues bringing profit.

5. The price to leave the market in case of unfavorable market changes (stop loss level).

The trading is made by a certain fixed volumes that are called lots. Usually1 lot is equal to 100,000 USD.

Here goes the example of a simple trade when US dollar is traded in Swiss franks:

OPEN BUY 1 LOT USD @ 1.3450

CLOSE SELL 1 LOT USD @ 1.3650

200 pips profit was gained (about 1,500 USD).

Many speculative trades on Forex are made on the principle of margin trading. The essence of this principle is the following: one does not need the whole lot sum for the trade, only a small part of the lot (called margin).

The margin usually makes 1-10% from the sum of the lot. When you wish to make trade operation, your financial partner (brokerage company) credits you with the necessary sum, or as the traders say "gives you the leverage". For example, when you wish to buy 100,000 US dollars for Swiss franks with1% margin, you should pay only 1,000 USD. When the position is opened, after a certain period of time, you should close the position.

Special trading systems, precisely defining the key moments of trading process, are made for systematic and successful trades.

Disclaimer

BONUS

SIMPLE TREND LINE: The above hourly GDP chart shows an excellent opportunity

to enter a short position on a trend line break of a previously strong upward trend.

The line ascending from the cycle low pivot point at point A identified a zone of support

all the way to point B. This trend line was actually formed by joining point A to the next

cycle low pivot point half way between points A and B. I'm sure you can see this on the

chart above.

Had we also connected the cycle high pivot points, this would have depicted an upward sloping

channel, bounded by the A-B trend line and the upper channel line. But, we

merely wanted to show the power of drawing trend lines driven by the prevailing

momentum of price action.

Once price broke through support at point B, the trend line quickly reversed roles and

identified a zone of resistance, as potential sellers took advantage of subsequent rallies to

sell the GDP. The same commentary applies to the lesser trend line to the right.

Using trend lines like this also provides unique opportunities to execute crystal clear exit

strategies.

Stop what you're doing for a minute and consider this. We'll show you how you

can get your share of the $6 trillion-a-day markets. You'll think you've died and gone to

Heaven when you find out how easy it is to mimic the pros.

Every day, six trillion dollars float through the hands of people who aren't any smarter

than you or I are. It doesn't make any difference if you're an accountant, baker, butcher,

retired sea captain, homemaker, airline pilot, surgeon - or cop on the beat.

If you're willing to take some direction, you deserve a nice piece of the action. You'll never have to learn zip about currencies. You will learn the techniques and strategies to go out and claim what is rightfully yours.

Play right along with the giants of world commerce. You won't be on the outside looking in; you'll be enjoying the thrill of a lifetime, riding on their king-size coattails. Trading the forex market deserves your serious consideration.

Forex trading has enjoyed exponential growth and widespread popularity over the past few years. It is only now that online foreign exchange trading is starting to get noticed. Until recently, large international banks were the big dogs in the foreign exchange (FX or forex for short) market, selectively allowing access via telephone trading to Fortune 1000 companies, large funds, high-net worth individuals, etc..

But now, there are online trading firms that provide individual traders like you and I with direct access to the largest, most liquid financial market in the world – the forex.

A lot of traders seem oblivious to this market. This unfamiliarity is the root cause of misconceptions about this exciting market.

Spot foreign exchange is the ideal market for active trading - more leverage than equities/futures/options. The market is highly volatile, has a tendency to trend strongly, and actively trades 24 hours per day. There are no limitations on when one can short a currency. Currency traders can make money when a currency is becoming stronger or weaker.

People think that life is a linear progression, which you go from A to B to C and so on. In fact, it's a total illusion, because anyone who thinks carefully about his/her own life knows that the pattern of his past is absolutely accidental and serendipitous. The key challenge in life is not to know where you are going, but prepare your character so when those wonderful moments of serendipity occur, you can listen to your heart and know what it is you need to do. Trading the forex is just another serendipitous moment in the course of your life. You will either embrace the opportunity or let it go. By the time you have finished reading this e-book, we believe you will not let this opportunity pass you by.

If you really wanted to learn how to trade the forex successfully, where would you go? Who would mentor you? Who would teach you? Who would show you how to take advantage of the market, instead of the other way around - the market taking advantage of you? If you could get there on your own, you'd already be there. We're here to help you conquer the magnificent world of forex trading.

The ideal market for trading …

Tired of giving money to your broker and feeling broker? Well, outperform him or her. Currencies don't crash. They outperform stocks. Earn immediate income and stop worrying about job security and layoffs forever.

WHY YOU SHOULD GIVE THE FOREX A SERIOUS LOOK

¾ Large returns

¾ Currencies trend well.

¾ There are no commissions.

¾ US$6 trillion a day and growing

¾ The forex is a very efficient market.

¾ High leverage: Each pip is worth US$10

¾ There is lots of movement in this market.

¾ You can trade 24X5 from home or anywhere.

¾ Little capital is required – as little as US$500.

¾ You can easily start out by taking 20 pips a day.

¾ You can trade whether you have a day job or not.

¾ You can hedge at FX Solutions. Not all market makers allow this.

¾ All you need is an Internet connection; charting/dealing software is free.

¾ This is real-time trading; 2.5 to four second response time; rare re-quotes.

¾ Low lot size: 100 to one ratio; US$100 controls US$10,000 (1,000 = 100,000)

RISKY YOU SAY?

Is forex risky business? Comparing trading the forex to other forms of trading, you will find that from a risk/reward standpoint, forex trading provides respectable returns.

The currency (foreign exchange) market is the largest and oldest financial market in the world. It is also called the foreign exchange market, or "FOREX" or "FX" market for short. It is the biggest and most liquid market in the world, and it is traded mainly through the 24 hour-a-day inter-bank currency market - the primary market for currencies. The forex market is a cash (or "spot") inter-bank market. By comparison, the currency futures market is only one per cent as big.

Foreign Exchange simply means the buying of one currency and selling another at the same time. In other words, the currency of one country is exchanged for those of another. The currencies of the world are on a floating exchange rate, and are always traded in pairs - Euro/Dollar, Dollar/Yen, etc. In excess of 85 percent of all daily transactions involve trading of the major currencies - Australian Dollar, British Pound, Canadian Dollar, Japanese Yen, Swiss Franc, and the U.S. Dollar.

Unlike the futures and stock markets, trading of currencies is not centralized on an exchange. Forex literally follows the sun around the world. Trading moves from major banking centres of the U.S. to Australia and New Zealand, to the Far East, to Europe and finally back to the U.S.

In the past, the forex inter-bank market was not available to small speculators due to the large minimum transaction sizes and often-stringent financial requirements. Banks, major currency dealers and the occasional huge speculator used to be the principal dealers. Only they were able to take advantage of the currency market's fantastic liquidity and strong trending nature of many of the world's primary currency exchange rates.

Today, foreign exchange market maker brokers such as FX Solutions are able to break down the larger sized inter-bank units, and offer small traders the opportunity to buy or sell any number of these smaller units (lots). These brokers give virtually any size trader, including individual speculators or smaller companies, the option to trade the same rates and price movements as the large players who once dominated the market. Market makers quote buying and selling rates for currencies, and they profit on the difference between their buying and selling rates.

THE SYSTEM

Forex Intraday Pivots Trading System

This is a trading system that I use primarily on the Swiss Franc (USD/CHF) in the Spot Foreign Exchange market. I will outline the system as I apply it to the Swiss Franc, hereafter known just as USD/CHF (I believe this stands for Confederation Helvetica Franc).

YOU NEED

1. Five-minute and 1-hour charts for the forex currencies. The 1-hour chart helps define

the intraday trend and the five-minute is used for entry and exit. I use MG Forex's charting package because their charts represent broker prices and closely reflect the prices of all retail brokerages (i.e., MG Forex, FX Solutions, FXCM, GFT Forex, Gain Capital, etc.).

I used to use premium charting packages such as WebTrader, Comstock and so on, but I found that the charts reflected prices that no retail FX broker in the world was quoting. Therefore, when watching support and resistance points (pivots), I would see the price shoot way beyond the support or resistance, and it would look like the point had been broken, when in reality it was just a price quote that was out of line with the filtered quotes that brokerages use. When using charts that reflect brokerage prices, you have a better idea of where you are.

Regarding the bar or candlestick charts, they both update every 2 1/2 minutes rather than tick-by-tick. Some people prefer this, because it keeps them from making decisions until they actually have a close of a bar or candlestick. As far as I know, they are both the same, updating every couple minutes, unless you hit the refresh button.

Lately, I have been calculating the pivot numbers at 3 pm EST, and then again at 12 am EST just to note the difference. Most of the time the numbers are pretty close, and in the same area. I go with the 12 am EST if there has been any significant movement since 3 pm EST, or if for some reason the numbers don't seem to be matching up with the price action.

Indicators: The 9 and 18 Exponential Moving Averages on both the 5-minute and 1-hour charts. The MACD on both the 5-minute and 1-hour charts.

3. Pivots calculator or pivots calculation which provides not only the Pivot, R1, R2, S1, S2, but also the M1, M2, M3, M4 points as well. It is common to find many

commodities futures traders calculate only the Pivot, R1, R2, S1, S2 points. Often, in the forex market, these minor points of support and resistance are very significant, and most of the time there seems to be no difference in their significance.

There is some difference in which 24-hour time frame to use to compute the daily open, high, low, close numbers. EST seems to have the best consistency for the forex market. I believe the reason is because this coincides with the opening of the Australian, New Zealand markets, which technically represent the first markets of the day to open, followed by the Asian, then the European, and finally the U.S. market.

There is one exception to my usage of this time frame. At 3 pm EST, I will calculate the new Pivots based on the completed 24-hour period, and if the prices move up or down significantly during the Australian and Asian sessions so that they come close to exceeding the R2 or S2 numbers before the start of the European session, I will recalculate them at 2400 GMT (8 pm EST), or even later at 12am EST. This way I have a fresh set of pivot numbers for the European and U.S. market sessions, which I trade.

The latest numbers for daily volume in the Global Foreign Exchange market say that between 2 trillion and 7 trillion dollars a day change hands! This is up from the normally quoted numbers of 1.5 trillion and 2 trillion. Because of this, even time frames such as the late U.S. market hours and early Australian and Asian time frames are producing significant market movement. A year or so ago these time frames produced very little market movement, and were not usually the best times to trade, but that is changing. I trade from the Frankfurt opening (11 pm PST) or the London opening (12 am PST) to 9 am PST, the mid-point of the US market time frame. This normally produces profitable market movement.

At 11 pm PST, I see where the prices are located. Generally, they have not moved too much since 3 pm EST, and I await a fresh break of one of the pivot numbers. The times on the charts that I use for illustration purposes are Eastern Standard Time. Therefore, 2 am on the charts is the beginning of the time frame I use.

HOW THE SYSTEM WORKS

I. The Set-Up

After you have calculated the pivot numbers for the day, place horizontal lines on your 5-minute and 1-hour charts at the pivot numbers for the day, or at least as many lines as your chart gives you room for. It should look something like this:

The lines in the above illustration represent five of the nine calculated numbers. On this five-minute chart, that was all there was room for. The nine numbers are:

There are several basic ways to trade pivot numbers. Some look for the prices to move to the higher end, and then sell in the upper third of the scale, or buy in the lower third of the scale of numbers (S1, M1, and S2).

However, in forex, the number of pips (points) that the currency will move in a 24-hour period is usually substantial. This means that a move from the pivot or even the M2 number down to S2, M1, or S1 could represent 40 to 100 pips. If this is true, in USD/CHF, that is worth between $272 to $680 per lot traded. Therefore, to ignore the move down from this area to the projected low of the day could represent losing out on a good opportunity.

Additionally, the currencies are the most trending markets in the world, and frequently they do not stop if they reach these lower levels. Therefore, to look to buy at these low points can be dangerous unless you have a clear reversal pattern in place, or some other criteria for a reversal being met.

Others look for a break of the pivot and trade it lower or higher to the S2 or R1 numbers, take a portion of the profit, and leave the rest anticipating a continued move to either S1 or R2. The system I use is an extension of this method of trading pivots. I will present the method in two parts. The first application is simply trading the pivots with NO INDICATORS. Then the second application is to utilize the MOVING AVERAGES and MACD. In this way, you will see that the most important aspect of the system is the relationship between price and the pivot numbers. Secondarily, and of lesser importance, are the indicators.

The reason for this is because indicators tend to lag behind the action. If you follow only indicators, you will frequently find yourself in "NO MAN'S LAND." This is that area in the middle between two points of support and resistance. The price can either continue on to the next point or reverse and go back to where it came from. This is the worst possible place to enter a trade, and yet that is where indicator trading often puts you. The best place to enter a trade is as close to support or resistance as possible. Obviously, if you are buying, you want to be sitting right on top of support and if selling, right below resistance.

The Trade

When price penetrates a pivot number, it often retraces back to the pivot, and touches it briefly. If it was support that was penetrated, and it does not move back up above it, but continues to hover just below it, there is about to be a drop in price. At the point that it retraces after dropping below support, enter a sell with a modest stop loss somewhere on the other side of the broken support line. Notice the illustration below of the USD/JPY at 2 am EST. The price had just broken below the S2 number, which was 123.38. It briefly touched the 123.38 to 123.41 area and then began to descend. As you can see, it moved down all through the European and US market sessions.

This USD/JPY trade exhibits a problem sometimes encountered. Price either moves higher than the R2 or lower than the S2 number. At that point, it is best to re-calculate the numbers, or monitor the trade based on its relationship to weekly pivot numbers.

FIBONACCI

The Fibonacci Sequence - The Secret to Market Movement

In his second book Nature's Law, Elliott refined his work to incorporate Fibonacci analysis. Since the beginning of his research, Elliott believed that the wave pattern he discovered was not the product of random chance, but of what he considered a "natural law" that was manifest in different facets of life. Indeed, we take the name of our market service from one of his observations:

"...the market has its law, just as is true of other things throughout the universe. Rhythm, or regular, measured and harmonious movement, is to be discerned. This law behind the market can be discovered only when the market is viewed in its proper light, and then is analyzed from this approach."

Through use of the Fibonacci sequence, Elliott attempted to identify the blueprint of that natural law.

Who was Fibonacci? Leonardo Fibonacci was a brilliant 13th Century mathematician from the city of Pisa, Italy. While that city is better known for its leaning tower, Fibonacci is much more significant to our modern evolution. It's thanks to him that we use the numerical system popularly called "Arabic," but which was more specifically the work of medieval Moslem mathematicians carrying on the mathematical traditions of the ancient Greeks and Egyptians. This system replaced the cumbersome and inefficient Roman numeral system, and added much needed refinements like decimalization, absolute values and other concepts that underlie our modern mathematics. If this was Fibonacci's sole contribution, it would still have been enough for its impact on western civilization. But this was only part of his contribution.

Much of Fibonacci's work is technical, and so we'll only summarize the key elements, particularly those that Elliott incorporated into the Wave Principle.

The Golden Ratio: The Golden Ratio (also called the Golden Mean or Golden Section) is based on the proportion 1.618-to-1, and its inverse .618-to-1. Through his research, Elliott found that the ratio was manifest in the design of natural structures (everything from snail shells to galaxies) as well as in human creations. The proportions are found to be pleasing to both the eye and ear. Another famous Leonardo, Leonardo Da Vinci, realized the ratio's significance in both art and science, and used it widely in his paintings and scientific drawings. The Ancient Egyptians used it in their art and architecture, including the building the of pyramids. Their contemporaries in what became Latin America also knew the ratio and used it in constructing the ancient pyramids found in Mexico and Peru. After thousands of years, these remain some of the most impressive engineering feats in human civilization. Because the Golden Ratio has a mathematical basis, Elliott felt the Wave Principle was built upon the same basis, and that the stock market, with its statistical records, was a natural place to look for it in action.

The Fibonacci Sequence: In addition to the Golden Ratio, the Fibonacci Sequence (or Summation Series, as Elliott called it) became an integral part of the Wave Principle, and is used in both wave ratio analysis, and in analyzing relationships between waves with respect to price and time. The Sequence is derived from the following observations Fibonacci made: The sum of any two adjacent numbers forms the next higher number in the sequence; e.g. 0+1=1, 1+1=2, 1+2=3, 2+3=5, 3+5=8, 5+8=13, 8+13=21, 13+21=34, 21+34=55, 34+55= 89, 55+89=144 -- and on into infinity. In this sequence, he also observed the following relationship between the sequence numbers: The ratio of any number to the next higher number is approximately .618 to 1, and to the next lower number 1.618 to 1. Between alternate numbers in the sequence, the ratio is approximately .382, whose inverse is 2.618.

These might be considered "primary" Fibonacci ratios. There are secondary and even tertiary ratios that are useful in trading, which I discuss below in more depth. Before we continue, though, I should say a few words about sentiment, which, in effect, is what produces wave patterns, and is the engine behind what we might call the "Fibonacci Effect."

Sentiment

Elliott contended there was an order in the market, and that it reflected natural cycles in human nature. Some academicians and others dispute that there is any "order" to the market, much less something so seemingly esoteric as "natural human cycles." However, an experienced application of Elliott Wave directly challenges their view. The advent of Fractal Analysis as popularized by Benoit B. Mandelbrot also has a Fibonacci basis and corroborates Elliott's principle, as does the work of Gann and Sklarew.

People, like the changes of the seasons, go through their cycles. We know this based on bio-rhythm research conducted over thirty years ago, which showed human beings do, in fact, go through emotional peaks and troughs, sexual peaks and troughs, physical peaks and troughs, and intellectual peaks and troughs that recur cyclically as the human organism renews itself. This apparently happens individually and en masse. When applied to the market, the effects of "news" are more likely to be determined by the sentiment then prevailing, than the particular event itself. Indeed, the record shows that trends in progress continue to their completion despite periodic reversals, and regardless of news events (whether good or bad) that occur in between. This is perhaps less obvious when viewed day-to-day, but very obvious when viewed in historical context. We've frequently seen cases where stocks have sold-off despite a report of good earnings, as well as the opposite case, where stocks experienced ridiculously high valuations when the fundamentals didn't justify them. These contradictory actions show the emotionally charged nature of the market, and how important, therefore, an understanding of sentiment is to trading. Wave analysis, combined with Fibonacci analysis, provide a mathematical roadmap to marking these sentiment swings.

Trading The Market With Elliott & Fibonacci

Below are examples of how these concepts are applied in practical trading, including some examples from my personal trading.

Retracement Ratios: Waves tend to retrace either exactly, or in relationship to, a Fibonacci ratio. As we discussed earlier, "primary" retracement ratios include , .382, .50, .618, 1.0, 1.618, and 2.618. These are also commonly expressed in percentage terms.

Secondary and Tertiary Retracement Ratios: Some of these include...

.786, the square root of .618. Retracements will commonly fall in the .77-.786 range.

2.236, is the square root of 5, the most important number in the Wave Principle and key to the composition of the Golden Ratio (2.236 + 1)/2= 1.618; (2.236 -1)/2= .618.

Similarly, retracements of .236 (.6183) are also prevalent, especially in corrective waves. Our work at Market Harmonics has also found .89 (the square root of .786) to frequently occur in deep retracements.

The value of these ratios is that taken with correct wave labeling, the ability to forecast price targets can be amazingly accurate.

Impulse Wave Relationships: We noted previously that in impulse waves, the non-extended waves (usually 1 & 5) will tend towards equivalence in length and time of formation. Since wave 3 is generally the longest wave, it will often (though not always) be 2.618 the length of waves 1 and 5. Where the waves are not of the same length, a Fibonacci relationship usually exists between them. Similarly, a Fibonacci relationship generally exists between waves 2 and 4 in the cases where one of the waves exceeds the length of the other. Finally, wave 4 often divides the entire impulse sequence by the Golden Ratio.

Corrective Wave Relationships: In 3-wave corrections, we look particularly for Fibonacci relationships that exist between waves A and B, and waves A and C. In A/B relationships, B will often be shorter, especially in a zigzag, with Fibonacci retracements of .382, .50 and .618 the most common. In a flat, B can be equivalent or even a bit longer than A. In A/C relationships, C is generally equal to or greater than A in length, and in cases where it is longer (or shorter) will generally be related to A by a Fibonacci ratio, most commonly .618. In an irregular (or expanded) flat correction, wave C can exceed A by as much as 1.618 or 2.618. In triangles (and as another example of the alternation guideline) at least one wave is related to its alternate by .618, or occasionally .786 (i.e.., wave A with C, B with D, or C with E).

Time Considerations

Elliott Wave analysis will usually forecast price targets either exactly or within points of a target. Where it can be more challenging is with time estimates. Elliotticians generally believe that time is secondary to wave form. But there are clues in the wave pattern and Fibonacci sequence that will help narrow the time frame for a significant trend change with reasonable accuracy.

One way is the actual waves themselves. If you are tracking, say, the conclusion of a wave 5, knowing that it should be equivalent to wave 1, or related in length by a Fibonacci ratio, you can apply the same forecast to time as well as price. For example, let's say wave 1 took 10 days to form. You might project wave 5 to take 10 days to also form. If wave 5 exceeds wave 1 in its formation, look for potential tops in roughly 13, 16, to 18 days. If on the other hand wave 5 appears to be losing steam on declining volume and may end up being shorter than wave 1, look for a possible reversal between 5-8 days from the start of its formation. I use days in this example, but the same can be true of months or years.

Occasionally, numbers in the Fibonacci sequence that coincide with dates for previous key market reversals can help in forecasting future ones. I used this method in helping to track turns in what then appeared to me the early phases of a bull market in oil and natural gas in March 2000 (right as techs were starting their nosedive). I discuss this, along with the application of the Wave Principle, in some examples from my personal trading.

First, I looked for past Fibonacci relationships between previous dates of significance (anywhere from 34, 55, 89, 144 or 233 days) and looked for any repetitive patterns based on these numbers. I also looked for where two or more of these dates converged over a similar time frame. This method assisted me in clarifying my wave count, and told me when to go longBand when to go short the XNG and XOI indices, which I did successfully over the next severalBmonths. The method isn't full proof by any means, though it seems the greater the number of relatable dates, the better its chance for timing potential changes.

I also incorporated this method in trading option contracts on the OEX (the S&P 100 index). I noted in my analysis a convergence of Fibonacci dates in the OEX around November 25, 2000 right in the middle of a two day rally following the Thanksgiving holiday. The foreknowledge allowed me to go short the index with option put contracts, as I expected a market decline to occur into early December. The OEX did indeed peak on November 27 (the first available trading day after the holiday) and declined until November 30, yielding me a nice profit on my options.

I had also projected two more potential time opportunities for the OEX (one to go long, one to go short) first on December 3-4, and then on or by Dec. 13. Below, I include my work charts from this period. I hope you'll please excuse the coffee stains and chicken-scratch, as these were actual working charts.

I labeled this chart on December 5 right at the start of what turned out to be a nice rally. I wasn't sure at the time, though, how much legs it would have, as I was trying to resolve the wave count from the 684.30 bottom on Nov. 30. I drew a trend line connecting two recent highs as a test, as I studied the wave pattern from the beginning of November, and noted that the overall pattern looked "corrective" and dominated by "threes". At the same time, there was a clear impulse wave up that had formed from the 684.30 bottom, suggesting a still incomplete upward correction that would very likely test and violate the trendline. And, it was consistent with the time estimate for a short-term rally. The figures beneath where I wrote "Upside Targets" shows my calculations for upward price targets and resistance areas using Fibonacci ratios. At this point, the index had yet to achieve even the first level .382 retracement. Another possible top was just above the 736 area, where there was a Minute Wave ii that I labeled. You'll also notice a couple of other labelings I made. The "(2) or (B)" note refers to a top on November 8 in a much larger and unfinished wave correction in the OEX. Some of my other notations indicate my tracking of this still incomplete declining wave.

Here I show a 15 minute chart of the results two days later. The 15 minute chart allowed me to get a better snapshot of the near term action. As you can see, the rally did, in fact, have legs, and confirmed my earlier forecast in November. When the OEX broke through my original trend line, I was in the market with some option call contracts to profit from the upside. You'll also see here that much more of the pattern is revealed, and I adjusted my original labeling to account for the wave action. I saw what appeared to be a wave 3 breakout, and the subdivisions of the wave appeared just as impulsive. If you remember from the first chart, the .618 retracement I calculated called for resistance at 731.36. Although it's not that clear on the chart, the index peaked at 732.79 and then reversed. I was happily out of the market at that point, having benefited from a 20 point index rise. Finally, I also calculated the potential length of what I considered to be a wave 4 pull back in progress. Using the Fibonacci ratios, I found support for wave 4 at 710 and then 707. If the index had broken below 707.46, it would have invalidated my count, since the 4th wave would have overlapped the 1st, violating one of Elliott's rules. It actually found support right in the middle, at 708, which kept the count valid. This also made wave 4 about even with the length of wave 2, and not surprisingly, just as wave 2 took 1 day to complete (Dec. 2 & 3 fell on a weekend) so did wave 4.

Here we see the last stage of this rally on a 30 minute chart. You'll note that wave 5 topped at 737.18, surpassing the wave 3 high, and falling a little short of the .786 retracement. It was, however, right in the range of the previous Minute Wave ii just above 736, which I had also considered a potential top. That, and the overbought condition of the technical indicators above the chart, told me the rally was running out of steam. Also, all the impulse waves (1, 3, & 5) were in relationship to each other by either the 50% or .618 retracement ratios, another head's up. Finally, you'll see the trend channel that I drew. Elliott stated that a parallel trend channel drawn from the peak of wave 1 through the base of a vertical wave 3 will often reveal the likely top for wave 5. That was certainly the case in this instance. In all, it was enough to tell me the rally had ended -- right on December 12. My next move? Position for option put buying to profit from the imminent decline.

Other Practical Considerations

Frost and Prechter noted that the Wave Principle works best with index trading, and to a lesser extent, stocks. Their view was that since the Wave Principle measures mass psychology in the market, individual stocks (and some commodities) didn't always provide reliable wave patterns for trading. After some years of putting Elliott to practical use in trading, I think their view is still generally true, though the market landscape has changed in some significant respects since their book was written. For one, there are individual stocks today that trade in higher daily volumes than the entire Dow Jones Industrial Average in the 1970's. Futures market volume has also increased dramatically, with the CME reporting the highest contract volumes in its entire history being reached in 2001. Consequently, I've been able to trade stocks pretty successfully using Elliott, though I usually won't bother with those that don't trade at least a million shares daily, or offer little volatility, since this helps produce good, readable waves. In my experience, that, in combination with other technical indicators, and a look at the fundamentals work well with using Elliott to trade high volume stocks.

I know that some Elliotticians and technicians turn their noses up at fundamentals. In the case of individual stocks, a look at fundamentals is justified for a few different reasons. First, it's an insight not only into the thinking, but also the sentiments of fundamental analysts towards a stock. For instance, valuations are key in gauging the relative value of a stock, and a stock with a low earnings yield and high P/E is doomed to correct, no matter what the touts tell you. Secondly, it's consistent with Frost and Prechter's view that the circumstances of a particular stock are just as likely to be affected by individual factors as technical factors. Third, such information is so freely available nowadays, it's silly not to look at fundamental analyst estimates, even if your ultimate decision is contrarian. Martin Pring, one of my favorite technicians (and one of the best out there) recommends that a wise trader take a "weight of evidence approach" to trading. After all these years, it remains one of the best pieces of advice I've ever heard.

Conclusions

I'm sure to folks seeing this for the first time, the Wave Principle might appear somewhat complicated and difficult to follow. I've only provided the highlights of Elliott Wave analysis in these pages. When I first came to trading and looked at numerous trading systems, none offered the consistently accurate record of forecasting and analysis as the Wave Principle. Robert Prechter, the leading exponent of Elliott Wave analysis today, proved it's effectiveness after winning a series of trading championships in the 1980's, where he was up against some of the market's foremost traders, earning an impressive 400% on this trade.

Some of the most stunningly accurate major market forecasts have been made by Elliotticians, including Elliott's own remarkable forecast of the end of a bear market decline in the Dow from 1933-1935, which he forecast to the exact day in a telegram to his publisher. Elliott also accurately forecast the bull market during World War II and its decline well ahead of the actual events. When one considers that in Elliott's day he was making charts and calculations by hand, without benefit of all the computerized toys we take for granted today, and that he was 67 years old when he embarked on his career as a forecaster, his discoveries and accomplishments are all the more impressive. A. Hamilton Bolton, a leading Elliottician during the 1950'-60's and founder of the Bank Credit Analyst advisory service (BCA Research today) forecast in 1960 the Dow would reach 1,000 in 1966 (it had been trading in the 500-600 range for most of that period). On February 9, 1966, the Dow reached an all time high of 995, having peaked at just over 1,000 intraday. In their 1978 book "Elliott Wave Principle, " written during the depths of the seemingly endless 1970's bear market, Robert Prechter and A. J. Frost predicted a vibrant bull market would begin in 1982. The forecast also called for the bull market to crash in 1987. As we know, the end of 1982 saw the rise, seemingly from out of nowhere, of a powerful 5-year bull market that peaked with the market crash of 1987. With an understanding of the principles of Elliott Wave analysis, it becomes clear why such bold forecasts can be made.

A WORD ON PRICE … THE NUMBER ONE INDICATOR …

Price doesn't lie. It is simply the fact – a number that tallies up the transactions at the forex, where everyone who knows anything is forced to show their hands in the form of trades for the record. There is no place to run and hide. We may never know why people are buying or selling, but if they are doing it, their actions are surely reflected in price. We can never be certain about world affairs, and we don't have to be, since everyone who is in the know is already acting in the market, and price is a real-time measurement of worth.

My view is that technical analysis is not a tool to be used to "forecast" the future. I use it to gather information, and diagnose what the market is doing in the here and now. This allows me to prepare a road map and contingency plans so that I am ready for just about anything. I believe that it is important to look at the behaviour of price itself, rather than rely solely on indicators to provide buy/sell signals, as traders tend to make decisions triggered by price change. Essentially, all we need to know is if there is movement or sideways action. In the case of trending, we want to know how strong. If we are into a sideways pattern, we want to identify areas of potential trend change or breakout. The goal is to buy every dip in an uptrend, and sell every rally in a downtrend. In a consolidation phase, we want to wait patiently for some sort of movement. Remember the adage, "The trend is your friend!" The Law of Inertia states that an object at rest or in motion tends to stay that way, unless acted upon by some external force. The same could be said for commodities futures, currencies, markets, and stocks.

It's in the charts ...

I use charts to help me assess what's likely to happen next – to examine past price movements to forecast future price movements. This approach to trading is called technical analysis. Technical analysts are trend followers who interpret price movement via charts to determine tradable up or down trends.

To the extent that technical analysis works, it is because human psychology plays a big role in traders' decisions to buy or sell, and that hasn't changed much over the years. Convinced devotees don't really want to know anything about the world's fortunes or outlook, except for news as it relates to currencies. They believe that everything that is known about world fundamentals is already reflected in the price.

Momentum traders believe that price will move in the path of least resistance, and that that path is defined by the trend in the price.

Of course, if you have access to volume with your charting service, that is an equally important measure to pay attention to.

In the case of the forex, this is the one place where news pays. Knowing what's going on in the news on any given currency can certainly give you the edge with your trading. That is not the case with other markets, where news is generally considered just plain old noise.

Bottom line, you have to be able to read price action in order to truly understand where price is going. And, just how do you do that? By looking at price through a filter. If you look at price by itself without any reference points to compare it to, you will have no way of knowing what it is doing - where it has been, where it is, where it is going, in what direction, and how fast. You can certainly use indicators like MACD to confirm where price is going, and help you make your entry or exit decision.

But, ultimately you have to be able to anticipate the next move of price before the dumb money does, because they're the ones who usually catch the wave at the tail end of a move. We will look at one filter, and perhaps the only filter that works on the forex, in the coming paragraphs. Strap in and listen up closely. You are about to go for an interesting ride.

An important concept to get down at this point is the concept of breathing. Every tradable in the forex "breaths" so many pips on average every trading session. It's important to know this number entering a session because that is the maximum number of pips you can hope to carve out per lot with your skilful trading. How you get this number is explained a little bit later on in the section on pivot points.

Technical traders believe that prices are created in an efficient market. Accordingly, price represents fair value reflecting the impact of every single fundamental factor known by anyone, anywhere. Such traders don't care about the fundamentals that affected price behaviour. All they know is that price moved, and that there was a reason for it.

A price derived by this tug of war between the world's buyers and sellers represents a combined expression of their collective opinions. Price ultimately becomes the unanimous consensus of all people who step up to the plate, and put their money where their mouth is.

Prices created in such efficient markets are anticipatory. Traders respond to what they know to be true, and they take positions based on what they know. This is especially true of forward markets. Based on what is on the table in the present, what will tomorrow bring?

Here are some words of wisdom about forex trading:

Develop a trading plan: A well-defined trading plan is essential to success in forex trading. This plan should include your goals, risk management strategies, and entry and exit rules.

Manage your risk: Forex trading is inherently risky, and it's important to manage your risk carefully. Use stop-loss orders and position sizing to limit your losses and protect your capital.

Keep your emotions in check: Emotions can cloud your judgment and lead to impulsive decisions. Stay calm and rational when making trading decisions and avoid trading based on fear or greed.

Stay informed: Stay up-to-date with market news and economic events that could impact currency prices. Keep an eye on major economic indicators and news releases that could affect the forex market.

Learn from your mistakes: Trading is a learning process, and it's important to learn from your mistakes. Analyze your trades and identify areas where you can improve.

Practice patience: Successful forex trading takes time and patience. Don't expect to become a millionaire overnight, and avoid taking unnecessary risks in pursuit of quick profits.

Continuously educate yourself: Forex trading is a dynamic field, and there is always something new to learn. Keep educating yourself through books, courses, and other resources to stay on top of the latest trends and strategies.

Remember, forex trading is not a get-rich-quick scheme, and success requires discipline, hard work, and a willingness to learn and adapt. With the right mindset and approach, however, forex trading can be a rewarding and profitable endeavor.